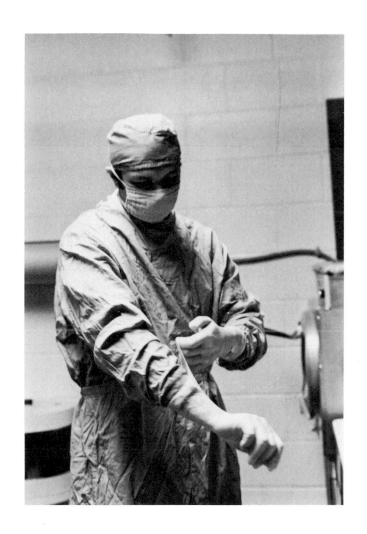

Behind the Scenes
at the Horse Hospital

Fern G. Brown

Behind the Scenes at the Horse Hospital

Photographs Roger Ruhlin

ALBERT WHITMAN & Company, Chicago

This book is dedicated to T. N. Phillips, D.V.M.; J. J. Foerner, D.V.M.; and the people who use their knowledge and skills behind the scenes at the Illinois Equine Hospital and Clinic to help horses live longer and healthier lives.

■

The author wishes to thank the following for help in preparation of this book: the American Association of Equine Practitioners; the American Veterinary Medical Association; Robert Baker, D.V.M., and Mike Hernandez, of the Chino Valley Equine Clinic, Chino, California; Thomas A. DeMeyer, D.V.M., and Jennie Becker of the DeMeyer Clinic, Grayslake, Illinois; the Friends of Handicapped Riders, Naperville, Illinois; William J. Lee, Jr., V.M.D., and Cindy Lee of the Pompano Equine Clinic, Pompano Beach, Florida; Robert McCullough, D.V.M., of Barrington, Illinois; Ben Schachter, D.V.M., and Michael Posner, D.V.M., of the Trail Animal Hospital, Delray Beach, Florida; Beryl Boettcher, Leonard J. Brown, Frances Lindstrom, Raymond Margolies, Ralph and Lillian Markus, Gail Peachin, Ann Penner, and Susan Rosalak for manuscript assistance.

With special thanks to T. N. Phillips, D.V.M., J. J. Foerner, D.V.M., and the entire staff at the Illinois Equine Hospital and Clinic, Naperville, Illinois.

Library of Congress Cataloging in Publication Data

Brown, Fern G.
   Behind the scenes at the horse hospital.

   Summary: Text and photographs present an account of life behind the scenes at the Illinois Equine Hospital.
    1. Horses—Diseases—Juvenile literature.
2. Veterinary hospitals—Juvenile literature.
[1. Horses—Diseases. 2. Veterinary hospitals]
I. Ruhlin, Roger. II. Title.

| SF951.B88 | 636.1'0832 | 81-94 |
| ISBN 0-8075-0610-9 | | AACR2 |

Contents

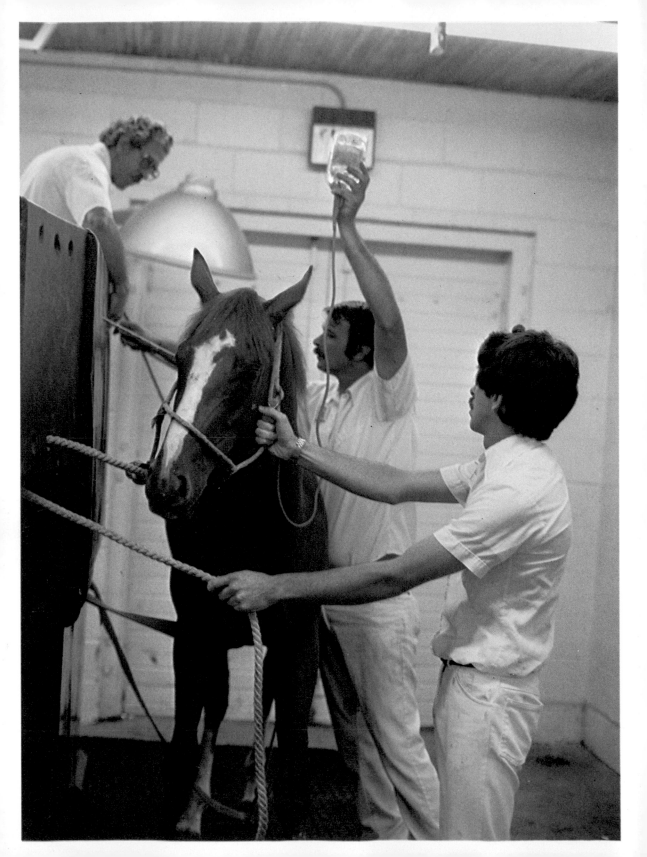

Helping Horses Live Longer

■

"He has to be put to sleep." These painful words aren't heard as often as they once were by owners of sick or injured horses. Let's look behind the scenes at an equine hospital, a hospital for horses, to see why.

Hospitals save lives

Ginger is a small, pretty, eight-year-old chestnut mare. When her eyes became watery and red, her owner called an equine veterinarian, a doctor for horses. The veterinarian examined the mare and prescribed medicine.

But after a week, when Ginger's eyes were still bloodshot and runny, her owner became alarmed. Ginger meant a lot to him and she wasn't getting any better. So he made an appointment at the Illinois Equine Hospital and Clinic in Naperville, Illinois, and took Ginger there in a horse trailer.

Ginger waited and Dr. T. N. Phillips

How do you lift a horse onto an operating table? The problem isn't so difficult if the table tilts. This patient at the Illinois Equine Hospital is being gently but firmly strapped to a tilting table while it is in an upright position.

was notified by the receptionist. He told the owner to take Ginger to the examining room.

After checking the horse and doing a complete blood count in the laboratory, Dr. Phillips took a sample of the diseased eye tissue. He sent the sample to a histopathologist at the Veterinary Diagnostic Medicine Center at the University of Illinois at Champaign-Urbana. A histopathologist is a doctor who specializes in studying abnormal cells.

Ginger was sent home to await the report. It was an anxious ten days for the owner. Then the report came back. Ginger had cancer!

Cancer is a scary word. It means cells are multiplying out of control, spreading and destroying the body. Ginger's case was unusual and frightening because the cancer was in both eyes. But there was some good news. Ginger's eyesight might be saved if Dr. Phillips removed the cancerous cells.

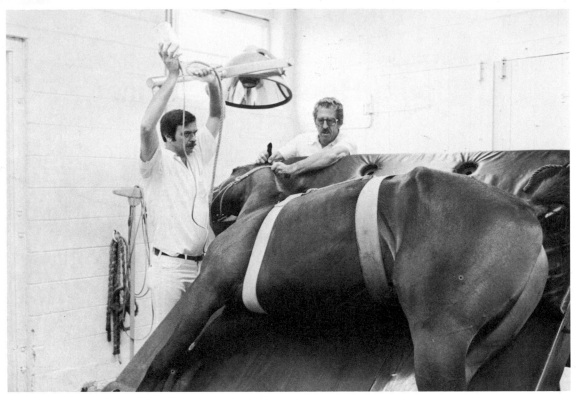

When the horse has been secured, the table is tilted to a horizontal position for the operation. The solution in the bottle is an anesthetic, which flows into the horse's veins. The anesthetic helps put the horse to sleep so it will not feel any pain during surgery.

We'll have to operate

The owner agreed to the surgery. Ginger was brought back to the hospital and assigned a large, clean stall which smelled of disinfectant. A barn worker gave Ginger feed and filled her water bucket. The little mare sniffed and pawed the bedding. Then she lay down and rolled. She seemed comfortable.

On the morning of the operation, Ginger was given a tranquilizer to keep her calm. After the shot, she was led to the large operating-room table.

Three veterinarians waited for Ginger: an anesthesiologist to give the anesthetic, Dr. Phillips to perform the surgery, and another veterinarian to assist Dr. Phillips. If the surgery had been more complicated, a fourth doctor would have been there, too.

The anesthesiologist gave Ginger an anesthetic so she would be asleep and feel no pain during the operation. Then while she was still standing, the doctors strapped her to the padded, metal operating table. They tilted the table so that Ginger was lying down. Soon she was fast asleep.

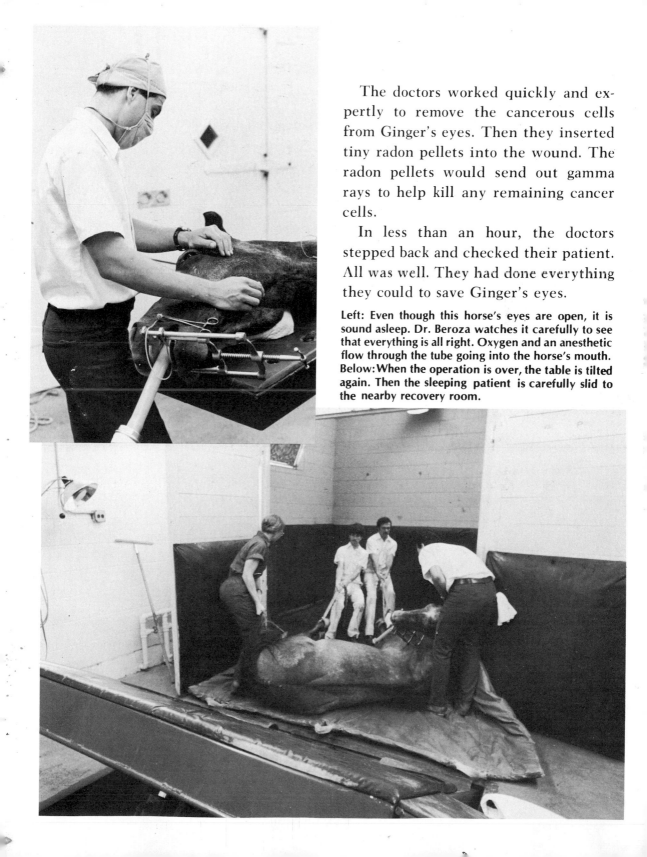

The doctors worked quickly and expertly to remove the cancerous cells from Ginger's eyes. Then they inserted tiny radon pellets into the wound. The radon pellets would send out gamma rays to help kill any remaining cancer cells.

In less than an hour, the doctors stepped back and checked their patient. All was well. They had done everything they could to save Ginger's eyes.

Left: Even though this horse's eyes are open, it is sound asleep. Dr. Beroza watches it carefully to see that everything is all right. Oxygen and an anesthetic flow through the tube going into the horse's mouth. Below: When the operation is over, the table is tilted again. Then the sleeping patient is carefully slid to the nearby recovery room.

Into the recovery room

The surgeons lowered and tilted the operating table. While Ginger was still asleep, they slid her gently through a passage in the wall to the padded floor of the recovery room next door.

About twenty minutes later Ginger awoke. She blinked her eyes, trying to focus. She wore no bandages because horses are apt to try to rub them off, **interfering with the healing process.** Ginger stared at the padded walls in the dark, windowless recovery room as if to ask, "What happened?" The anesthesiologist said a few soothing words and patted her neck.

As the anesthetic wore off, Ginger gave a loud whinny and tried to stand. She fell, but the special floor and padded walls kept her from getting hurt.

Soon the plucky little mare tried again. This time she managed to stand, although her legs were wobbly. Less than two hours later, she was back in her stall, contentedly munching hay.

Ginger stayed in the hospital for six

A sick horse needs tender, loving care. Dr. Beroza gives aspirin to a patient recovering from surgery.

days. The barn workers fed her and kept her stall clean. A veterinarian watched her and gave her medicine. Day or night, there was always a doctor in the hospital if Ginger needed extra attention. When she returned home, she made an excellent recovery.

An accident case

In the past, nasty barbed-wire cuts caused serious infections and were responsible for the deaths of many horses. Today animals injured by barbed wire can often be saved at equine hospitals.

Amara is a purebred Arabian mare kept for breeding on a Wyoming ranch. She was grazing in a field with her young colt, Julep, when a horse in the next pasture leaned over the fence and nipped Julep.

Amara was very protective of her colt. She raced excitedly along the fence and tried to strike out at the intruder. She bucked, kicked her hind legs in the air, and tore thirty feet of the top row of barbed wire from the fence. The wire wrapped around her left hind leg and made a large, ugly cut in the tendon in her hock, where the leg bends.

The leg soon stopped bleeding, but the cut was deep and needed stitching. Amara's owner called the veterinarian's office, and the office worker told her to bring Amara to the hospital before the wound became infected.

Exercise is critical for recovery, especially for leg and foot injuries. This patient is being exercised around the turnout at the Illinois Equine Hospital.

But how could Julep be left behind? The two-month-old colt would suffer if he were separated from his mother, and Amara would be terribly upset if the colt was out of her sight. So the owner loaded both horses in her trailer and drove to the Dayton Veterinary Clinic in Dayton, Wyoming, as fast as she could.

11

A brave mother and colt

Dr. Fred P. Hosking treated Amara immediately. He gave her a tranquilizer to calm her and a local anesthetic to dull the pain. Then he sewed up the deep cuts and scratches and repaired the hock area.

Amara was very brave. She stood in the surgery room without a whimper, never taking her eyes from her colt. It's hard to get young colts to stand still because they are so full of spirit and energy. But Julep stayed patiently in front of his mother for the entire three-hour ordeal.

During the last few minutes of surgery Amara became so restless that it was difficult for Dr. Hosking to bandage her leg. But with a few words of encouragement from her owner, she settled down.

Amara and Julep spent three days in the hospital. Now Amara can walk, trot, and canter in spite of her permanently swollen leg. Her circulation is poor because the lymph vessels in her leg were

What's going on here? The long, thin tube has been gently put through the horse's nose and down into its throat. Then the throat can be thoroughly examined as doctors look through the tube. This procedure is called an endoscopy.

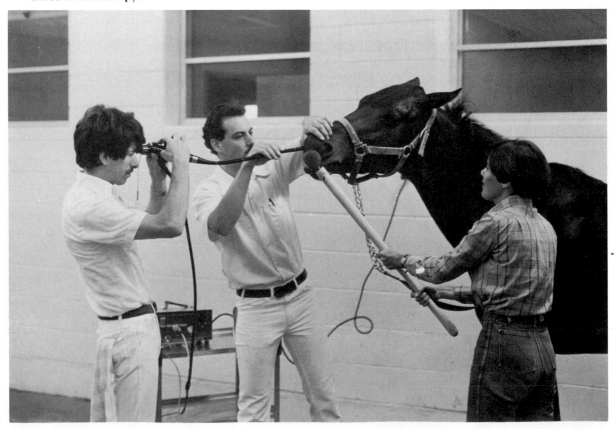

destroyed. But she's had three healthy foals since the accident. Without the expert care at the Dayton Clinic, the results might have been quite different.

Why horse hospitals are important

Ginger and Amara regained their health as a result of the combined efforts of the veterinarians, surgeons, laboratory technicians, pathologists, and various attendants who work behind the scenes in the equine hospital. These two cases might not have ended happily if the horses hadn't been taken to hospitals.

You may know people brought up on farms who remember the veterinarian coming out to perform surgery on a sick horse in the barn. That's the only way horses were treated in the past.

Today some veterinarians still make house calls. At the Illinois Equine Hospital there are seven veterinarians. Three go out on calls. But the majority of patients are brought to the hospital in trailers, as Ginger was.

In their home barns, horses might become infected because of dirt and germs. At an equine hospital, doctors work under well-lighted, sanitary conditions. Hospital operating rooms are always kept immaculately clean and disinfected.

Hospitals have special equipment that cannot be carried to stables. The operating table at the Illinois Equine

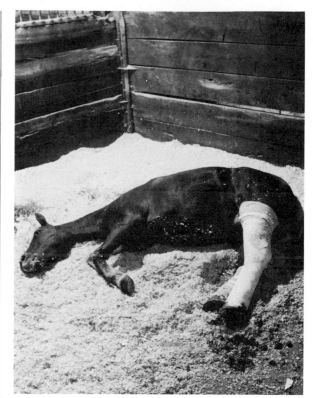

Lollipop, a pony with a broken leg, rests after her surgery. The cast stayed on Lollipop's leg for three months.

Hospital is six and one-half feet square and made of heavy steel. No doctor can carry around something like that!

At most hospitals, twenty-four-hour care is available. Often one of the veterinarians lives at the hospital.

Besides performing surgery, veterinarians at equine hospitals treat pneumonia, non-surgical colic, and diseases caused by parasites. They help mares who are having trouble giving birth. They set fractures, pull abscessed or infected teeth, and diagnose lameness and arthritis, a common disease which causes swelling of the joints.

Most patients who come to the Illinois Equine Hospital arrive in a horse trailer such as this one, pulled by a van.

Many kinds of hospitals

Equine hospitals vary in size. The Illinois Equine Hospital has twenty-one stalls; Dr. Tom DeMeyer's hospital in Grayslake, Illinois, has only four. The Chino Valley Equine Hospital in Chino, California, is a very large private hospital, with thirty stalls. There, Dr. Robert Baker, the owner, and his staff treat horses from all over the state as well as from the neighboring states of Arizona and New Mexico.

Besides these privately owned equine hospitals, there are many excellent veterinary hospitals and clinics attached to teaching colleges of veterinary medicine in the United States and Canada. One example is the New Bolton Center at the University of Pennsylvania in Philadelphia, Pennsylvania, where there are approximately seventy veterinarians on the staff and more than one hundred stalls.

Equine hospitals and clinics specialize in horses only, but some large animal hospitals, such as Trail Animal Hospital in Delray Beach, Florida, also treat cattle and other animals.

14

A case of colic

Not all veterinarians are surgeons. Those who aren't refer patients who need surgery to hospitals. This is what happened in the case of a mare named Butterscotch, who had colic. Colic is a terrible bellyache.

Butterscotch refused to eat or drink. She was sweating heavily and was very restless. Her owner recognized the symptoms of colic, and he knew that without treatment Butterscotch could die. Many horses with colic die pain-fully due to shock or blood poisoning or peritonitis, an inflammation of the membranes lining the abdominal cavity.

The owner acted fast and called the veterinarian. An office worker relayed the call over a two-way radio to the doctor's mobile truck. Since it was an emergency, the veterinarian delayed his next appointment and hurried out to examine Butterscotch in her home barn. The doctor's mobile truck contained refrigerated vaccines, drawers of drugs and other medical supplies, and hot and

Sometimes other large animals make use of the special equipment and trained personnel at the Illinois Equine Hospital. This elephant had a fractured leg and needed surgery.

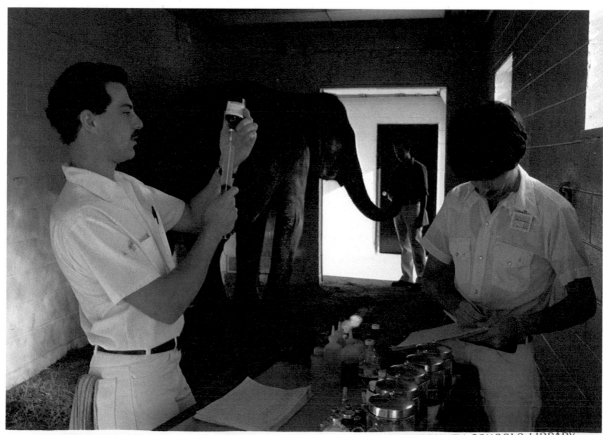

cold sterilized water for washing injuries. But he was not equipped to operate. He recommended immediate surgery in the equine hospital.

When Butterscotch's abdominal cavity was opened, the hospital doctors found the large colon blocked by ordinary sand. They removed four buckets of sand from the horse's colon!

It was later discovered that the sand was from the riding-ring floor, where Butterscotch had been fed during the winter. As she ate her hay, she also ate sand from the floor.

Although Butterscotch's veterinarian did not perform the surgery, he was allowed in the operating room. This is a courtesy usually extended to veterinarians, but not often to owners or trainers.

They don't shoot horses

At the Chino Valley Equine Hospital in California, seventy-five percent of the patients are racehorses. Several years ago, a famous Thoroughbred stallion who had raced in the Kentucky Derby broke his hind leg in a race. He was brought to the hospital from the racetrack.

There are many ways to find out if something is wrong with a horse. Here Dr. Phillips flexes a horse's front leg to help determine if the horse is lame. The owner helps keep the patient calm.

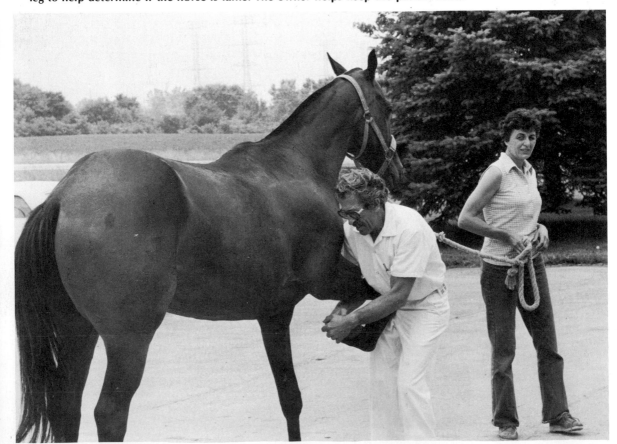

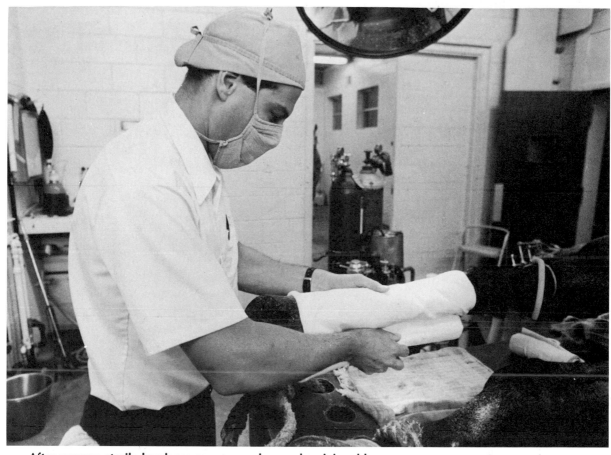

After surgery, sterile bandages are wrapped around an injured leg.

If you believe the old saying, "When a horse breaks his leg—shoot it," you'll have to change your thinking. Today doctors don't often shoot horses with broken legs. Most cases are handled with surgery.

The doctors hoped that the Thoroughbred's break was a common chip fracture of his knee or ankle and that they could repair it so the stallion could return to racing. But the X rays showed that the break was more complicated. Dr. Baker operated, using stainless-steel bone screws to fasten the fractured fragment of bone back to the main bone. The Thoroughbred never raced again, but he made an excellent recovery and sired many foals.

A valuable Canadian stallion show horse broke his right hind leg while at a horse show in the Chicago area. He was taken to Dr. Tom DeMeyer's hospital in Grayslake. The injury was serious because the bones were broken in several places close to the foot. The horse's leg was put into a heavy plaster cast;

Sometimes horses help people feel better. Like the lame pony who was treated at the Illinois Equine Hospital, this horse has been specially trained to carry handicapped riders.

then traction was applied to stretch and pull the bone fragments into line.

Since the horse's home was far away, and he was in no condition to travel, he stayed in the hospital. The cast was so heavy he had a difficult time limping around. He couldn't lie down, so he slept standing up. When he finally did manage to lie down, he couldn't get up again. But it didn't take him long to work out that problem. He learned to stand up like a cow, hind end first.

In spite of enormous pain, the stallion ate and drank and showed a strong will to get well. After five months in the hospital and three cast changes, he was able to walk without help.

The Canadian stallion survived the long trailer ride home. He's not entered in show competition any more, but he's still a good breeder, and he's sired several championship foals.

Not all leg problems are as serious as these. A pony who had suddenly gone lame was brought into the Illinois Equine Hospital. The doctors tested her leg on the grass, on gravel, and on pavement. They decided she had tendon trouble.

The pony had been schooled to carry handicapped riders, and a handicapped riding class needed her. Her leg was placed in a plaster cast for five weeks, and it repaired well. Now it's as good as new. The pony is once again the pet of the handicapped riding class.

Horses can be outpatients, too

Outpatients—patients who do not stay overnight—are also treated in equine hospitals. A horse can be brought in for examination and returned home on the same day. That's why many hospitals are also called clinics.

The Pompano Equine Clinic at Pompano Beach, Florida, has no stalls. Situated on the training grounds of the Pompano Park Racetrack, it treats mostly Standardbred horses that pull sulkies, light two-wheeled carriages. After any type of treatment, including surgery, the patient returns to the home stall on the backstretch of the racetrack.

Is this miniature horse real? Yes, and because it had colic, it was a patient at the Illinois Equine Hospital. The little animal is called a Fallabella. Fallabellas came originally from South America. They grow to be only about thirty inches tall.

Veterinarians sometimes refer their patients to a hospital or clinic for consultation. They discuss the case with the hospital doctors and get advice. Or veterinarians may send a copy of a case record to the hospital and discuss it with hospital doctors over the telephone.

Sometimes insurance companies that insure valuable horses insist on a second expert opinion when their clients' horses get sick or have an accident. So they consult with the expert veterinarians at equine hospitals.

When a sick horse is brought in for consultation, the doctors may simply discuss the treatment and medication that was first prescribed. Or the hospital doctor may take more X rays and do additional laboratory studies.

After carefully considering all the facts, the doctors tell the owner what they think is the best way to help the patient.

Many heads are sometimes better than one. Here Dr. Phillips and his staff examine some X rays and confer about treatment for a patient.

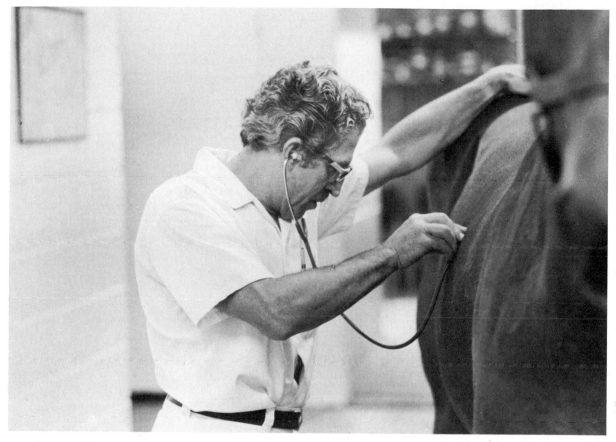

This horse has pneumonia. Dr. Phillips listens to its lungs to hear irregularities in breathing.

What if a horse can't be saved?

The horses you've just read about have made good recoveries. But there are times when the doctors have done everything they can and still the patient doesn't get well. If a horse cannot be helped, then it is destroyed as humanely as possible.

One horse that came to the Illinois Equine Hospital had a shattered knee that was not repairable. He was in terrible pain, and the kindest thing the doctor could do was to put him to sleep.

Another time doctors discovered during surgery that a horse with severe colic could not be saved. They knew she would suffer horribly for at least twenty-four hours and then die. So they injected a drug into her veins, and she slipped away peacefully.

Sometimes a necropsy, or examination of the body, is performed on a horse after it dies. A necropsy can help veterinarians determine the cause of death. It can also aid doctors in treating other horses with similar problems.

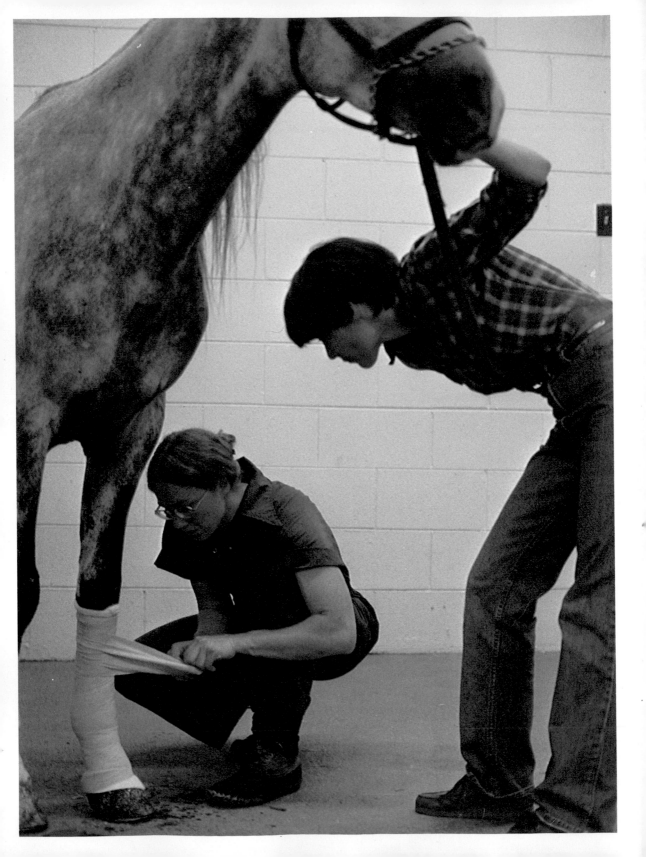

The Horse Hospital, Inside and Outside

■ ■

Equine hospitals provide their patients with the most comfortable environment and the highest quality equipment and care possible.

What does the hospital look like?

The Illinois Equine Hospital is a brick-faced building set on three acres. It is air-conditioned and has a reception area, several doctors' offices, two examining rooms, a laboratory, a pharmacy, twenty-one stalls, and an operating room with two recovery areas. There is also a barn in back of the hospital for storage of hay and shavings.

Some hospitals are not as big as the Illinois Equine Hospital; those connected with universities are much

How do things look? Dr. MacHarg removes a bandage to see if a patient's skin disease is clearing up, while a student watches.

larger. But no matter what the size, all equine hospitals try to have the very best equipment and the cleanest, safest surroundings for their patients.

The reception and surgery areas

With its desks and filing cabinets, the reception area at the Illinois Equine Hospital looks like a school office. Owners go there first to check in their horses.

After a horse is admitted to the hospital, it is taken to the examining room. In small hospitals patients are often examined in multi-purpose areas.

Surgical rooms have bright lighting because it's essential that doctors see clearly when they operate. The vinyl-padded metal surgical table at the Pompano Equine Clinic is fifteen-feet wide and eight-feet high—that's taller than the tallest basketball player. Although

It's impossible to be too particular about medicines. Here a prescription is being carefully filled at the pharmacy in the Illinois Equine Hospital.

all operating tables are not that large, they must be big enough to accommodate horses.

Straps similiar to seat belts in our cars bind the horse to the table. Everything possible is done to prevent injury during surgery. Horses sometimes wear protective hoods and leg bandages so they are completely cushioned. The surgical table can be folded and wheeled away when it is not in use.

After an operation, horses are taken to a nearby recovery room. There, padded walls and floors prevent patients from getting hurt if they fall.

The recovery room at the Trail Animal Hospital in Delray Beach, Florida, has an observation window made of shatterproof glass and covered with wire. Doctors can look in on patients without disturbing them, and there's no danger that the horses will break the glass and injure themselves.

The pharmacy

Almost all human medications, with the exception of experimental drugs, are used for horses. Equine hospital pharmacies are stocked with penicillin, cortisone, tranquilizers, painkillers, serums, ointments, and antihistamines.

Dr. William Lee, Jr., owner-veterinarian at the Pompano Equine Clinic, mixes and bottles his own ointments, lotions, and leg paints. One of Dr. Lee's preparations is called "337." Turn this book upside down and you'll see that the number "337" looks like his name.

Veterinarians also work to prevent illness. They stock their pharmacies with vaccines, vitamins, and other preventative medicines to help keep horses healthy.

The stalls

Most equine hospitals have roomy stalls. Those at the Illinois Equine Hospital have twelve-by-twelve feet of clay floor space. Wood shavings cover the clay and provide comfortable bedding for the horses. Metal bars enclose the upper half of the stall, making it easy for the doctors and barn workers to see the patients. Because mares and geldings usually get along well, their stalls face each other on the inside of the stall area. Spirited stallions are kept in outside stalls separated by solid partitions.

One or two stalls are used to isolate horses with infectious diseases such as strangles. Strangles is something like the strep throat that humans catch but more serious and highly contagious.

The Trail Animal Hospital in Florida has two isolation stalls. They are in a building separate from the main hospital. There, Dr. Ben Schachter and his partner, Dr. Michael Posner, recently treated a mare with strangles. The mare was put in an isolation stall as soon as the disease was diagnosed. The doctors listened to her chest and took her pulse several times a day. They saw her through the illness.

Because the mare was isolated as soon as the illness was identified, no other horse in the hospital became infected. When the mare went home, the isolation stall was steamed and sprayed with disinfectant to kill the bacteria.

The laboratory

Laboratories are used primarily for diagnostic purposes. Most hospitals try to do as much of their own laboratory work as possible so that they can quickly receive results. Routine blood work such as a Complete Blood Count (CBC) is usually done in the equine hospital laboratory. After the technician draws blood, the red and white cells are counted under a microscope. Small hospitals use a hand counter that looks like a stopwatch. Larger hospitals have a machine that automatically counts the cells. Both methods are accurate.

Cultures from urine, blood, or from a wound are also done in hospital laboratories. It usually takes forty-eight hours to find out what effect a particular

At the Illinois Equine Hospital, medicines are usually given out in the morning. It is critical that the right amount of each prescription be given to the right patient.

medication has on a disease organism, so it's important to get test results quickly and begin treatment as soon as possible. Many hospitals use sterile test kits complete with chemical slides, tubes and everything else necessary to perform a test. The kits save a lot of time and trouble.

As with humans, certain drugs may work better in one case than another. Although penicillin is a good all-around antibiotic, there are bacteria that resist it, so sometimes other antibiotics must be tried.

When laboratory work is complicated, equine hospitals often send samples from the wound or infection to better-equipped laboratories for diagnosis. Some hospitals rely on state laboratories at the Department of Agriculture or send their work to human laboratories. There are also a few private veterinary laboratories.

Sometimes samples of tissue removed during surgery are preserved in a tissue bank in a solution of formaldehyde and water. Veterinarians keep the samples so they can recheck their diagnoses. Or,

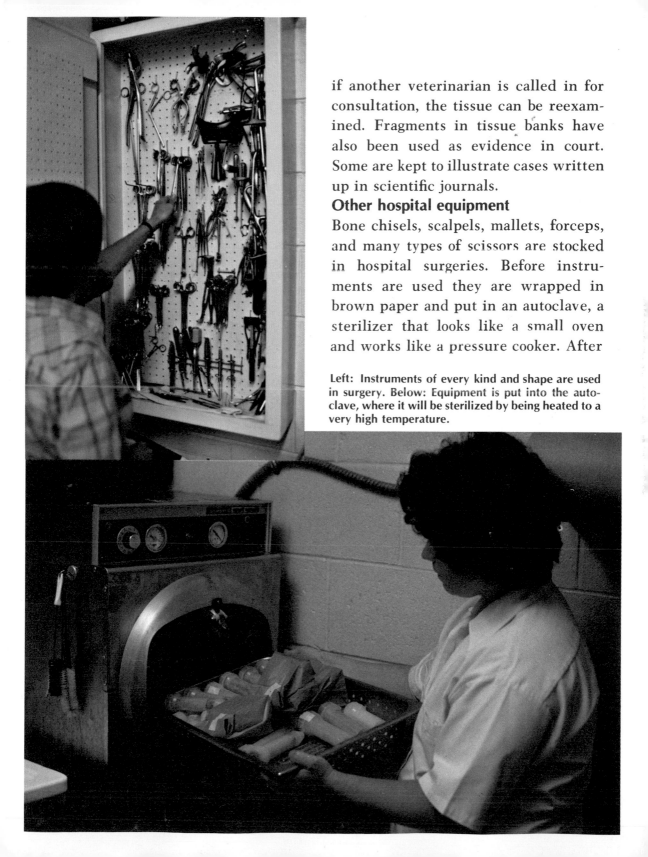

if another veterinarian is called in for consultation, the tissue can be reexamined. Fragments in tissue banks have also been used as evidence in court. Some are kept to illustrate cases written up in scientific journals.

Other hospital equipment

Bone chisels, scalpels, mallets, forceps, and many types of scissors are stocked in hospital surgeries. Before instruments are used they are wrapped in brown paper and put in an autoclave, a sterilizer that looks like a small oven and works like a pressure cooker. After

Left: Instruments of every kind and shape are used in surgery. Below: Equipment is put into the autoclave, where it will be sterilized by being heated to a very high temperature.

about thirty-five minutes in the auto-clave the instruments are sterile, or free from germs.

Oxygen tanks, cauterization machines to seal blood vessels, and other equipment used during surgery are also kept in the operating room.

One of the most important diagnostic tools for veterinarians is the X-ray machine. An X ray can show where a bone is broken, what is causing a horse to limp, or how far a disease has spread throughout the body.

Most hospitals have both stationary units and wall-mounted portable X-ray machines. Portable X-ray units can be used in any room of the hospital. They may even be taken outside of the hospital so that sick animals can be X-rayed in their own barns.

An X ray can be developed quickly, in less than two minutes. It is studied in a viewer by the veterinarian. Then a diagnosis is made and treatment is prescribed.

A gelding named Gilligan was lame for an entire year. The veterinarian treated him at his home stable and fi-

A patient is X-rayed. The doctors and other workers wear lead aprons to protect themselves from being exposed to too much radiation.

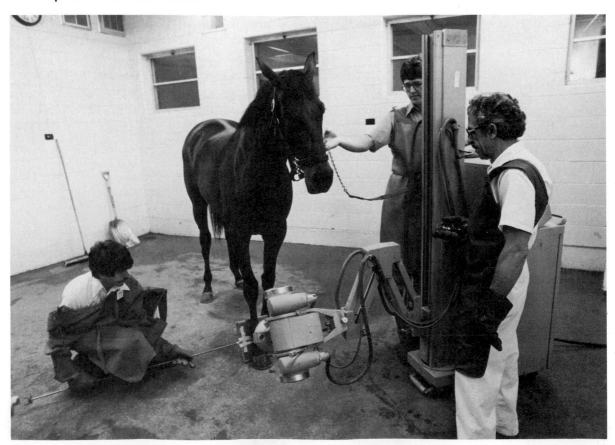

nally decided that surgery was needed. But before operating, the doctor suggested that the owner take Gilligan to the School of Veterinary Medicine at Purdue University in West Lafayette, Indiana, for a second opinion.

Although the trip took five hours, it was worth the trouble. Purdue University X-ray equipment is very advanced. A horse's back and spine can be X-rayed while the animal is lying down, the way human patients are often X-rayed.

The X ray helped the doctors decide that Gilligan needed corrective shoeing. The ferrier who had made Gilligan's shoes was told to taper the shoes to fit Gilligan's narrow hooves instead of tapering the hooves to fit the shape of the shoe. Sounds simple doesn't it? But several veterinarians took hours of testing and consultation to reach that decision. X rays were an important factor in the diagnosis which saved Gilligan from having to undergo surgery.

Outside the hospital

Many equine hospitals test horses for lameness on special outside surfaces such as blacktop or gravel tracks. In small hospitals, a lame horse may be examined by simply trotting it up and down the driveway.

Often horses are tested in turnouts, which are circular, fenced-in fields. At Illinois Equine Hospital there are two

X rays give important information. Here an X ray of leg bones is studied by a student.

large turnouts. Horses are put on a long rope called a lunge line and guided around the grassy enclosure.

The Pompano Equine Clinic has an unheated, oval-shaped swimming pool, fifty feet in diameter and sixteen feet deep. It is used for training and therapy.

Since most of the clinic's patients are racehorses, they often have ankle, leg, and shoulder problems caused by running on hard ground. Swimming relieves the pressure on bones and muscles. It builds up lung capacity and strengthens leg muscles.

A Standardbred racehorse with an acute knee injury was X-rayed, and the veterinarian decided that swimming would help the swollen knee.

An attendant cleaned the horse's feet and attached a rope to his halter. The horse seemed jittery and scared. He didn't like the pool, and when he hit the water he began to thrash wildly. The attendant stood in front of him and pulled the rope so the horse wouldn't turn on

his back and drown. Luckily, there was an emergency exit in the pool, and the terrified animal could quickly be pulled out.

The next day the patient was brought back to the pool. He was still too frightened to swim and had to be pulled out again. But on the third day he relaxed and swam several laps.

For a month the horse swam ten to twelve laps every day. The swelling subsided in his knee, and he went back to racing.

Many racehorses at the Pompano Clinic, especially those with arthritis,

A patient at the Pompano Equine Clinic receives therapy in the clinic pool.

Courtesy of the Pompano Equine Clinic

When the swimming session is over, the horse climbs up a special ramp to get out of the pool.

train daily in the swimming pool. They go from racetrack to pool, and their feet never touch the hard ground of the training track.

How much does it cost?

When Gilligan went to Purdue University as an outpatient, the owner paid twenty dollars for the doctor's services and thirty-six dollars for X rays. But a stay in an equine hospital can be much more costly, especially if surgery is involved.

The client must pay the examination, X ray, and diagnostic fees. In addition, there is a surgeon's fee and a charge for the operating room and anesthetic used during surgery. An operation to correct a simple chip-fracture costs hundreds of dollars. Complicated surgery is even more expensive.

There are also extra charges for medication and a daily board charge.

Although hospital care is costly, most owners feel that their money is well spent. They need the veterinarian, the trained staff, and the use of high-priced hospital equipment to keep their valuable and loved horses healthy.

31

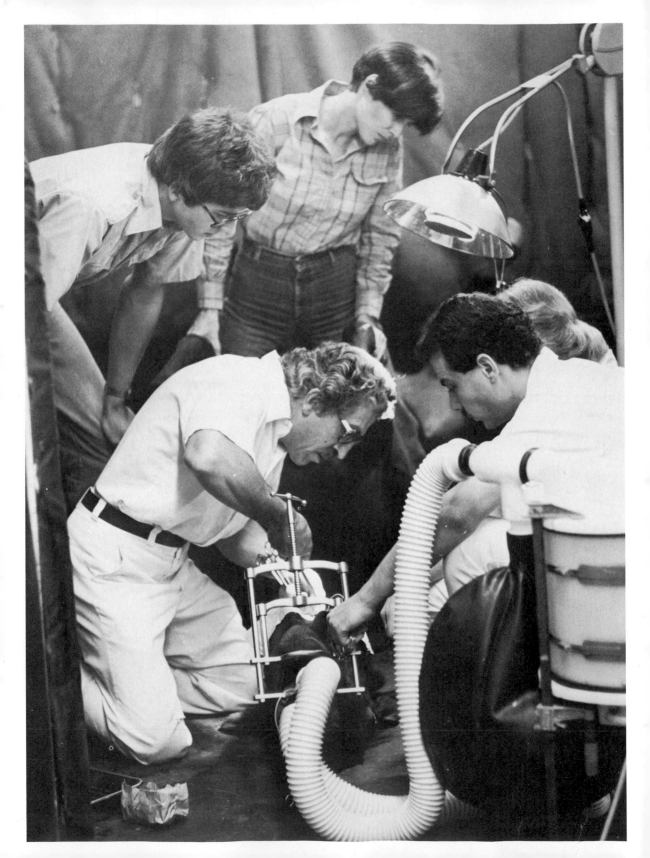

The Horse Hospital People

■ ■ ■

From the chief veterinarian to the barn workers, the people in the horse hospital use their knowledge and skill to protect the health and well-being of their patients.

The equine veterinarian

An equine veterinarian has a lot of responsibility. He examines patients, advises owners on ways to keep their horses healthy, and decides when to hospitalize horses. In order to make correct diagnoses and prescribe the right treatments, the veterinarian must have thorough knowledge of animal physiology and diseases. He must be highly skilled in the use of laboratory tests, X-ray machines, and other diagnostic tools.

At the Illinois Equine Hospital the chief veterinarian is Dr. T. N. Phillips.

Dr. Phillips removes an obstruction from a horse's larynx. The tube going into the horse's mouth provides oxygen and an anesthetic.

His staff consists of three hospital veterinarians and three other doctors who make house calls. Besides doing preventative, diagnostic, and surgical work, Dr. Phillips keeps records and tends to personnel problems and other business matters. He also supervises the part-time laboratory technician, three office people, the building engineer, and several barn workers.

Dr. Phillips' job isn't easy. He's at the hospital at 8 A.M. every morning and puts in at least a nine-hour day. Taking care of emergency patients often extends his day to twelve or more hours.

A veterinarian at a small equine hospital frequently does most of the work himself, helped perhaps by one or two assistants. The doctor is his or her own boss.

Although being the boss of your own hospital has advantages, it's very costly

33

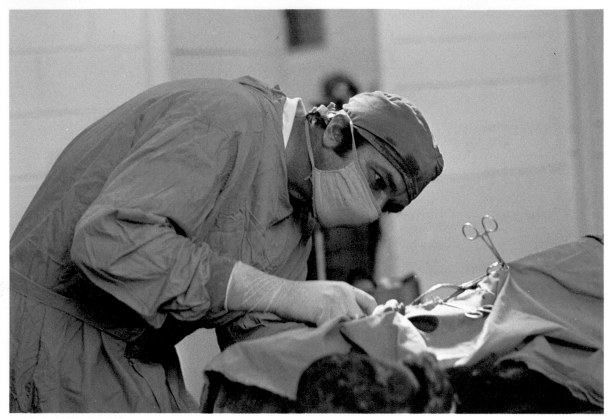

Surgery requires keen concentration, fine eyesight, and great manual dexterity. Dr. Foerner, of the Illinois Equine Hospital, wears an operating gown, cap, and mask to help protect the patient from germs.

to start a private equine hospital. A building has to be bought or built, and a lot of expensive equipment must be purchased, including a mobile truck. Establishing a veterinary hospital or clinic can cost hundreds of thousands of dollars, and prices keep going up.

Human community hospitals may receive some government tax money, but veterinary hospitals must be financed completely by the owner. Sometimes two or more veterinarians get together and share building costs. That's the way Dr. Phillips and his partners built the Illinois Equine Hospital. Their business went well, and ten years later they purchased more equipment and built a sizeable addition to the hospital.

Some veterinarians work at colleges or universities instead of having their own private practice. There the large volume of work is divided among dozens of veterinarians. Besides seeing patients at the clinic, experienced doctors teach classes in veterinary medicine.

Dr. Phillips gives one of his patients a shot.

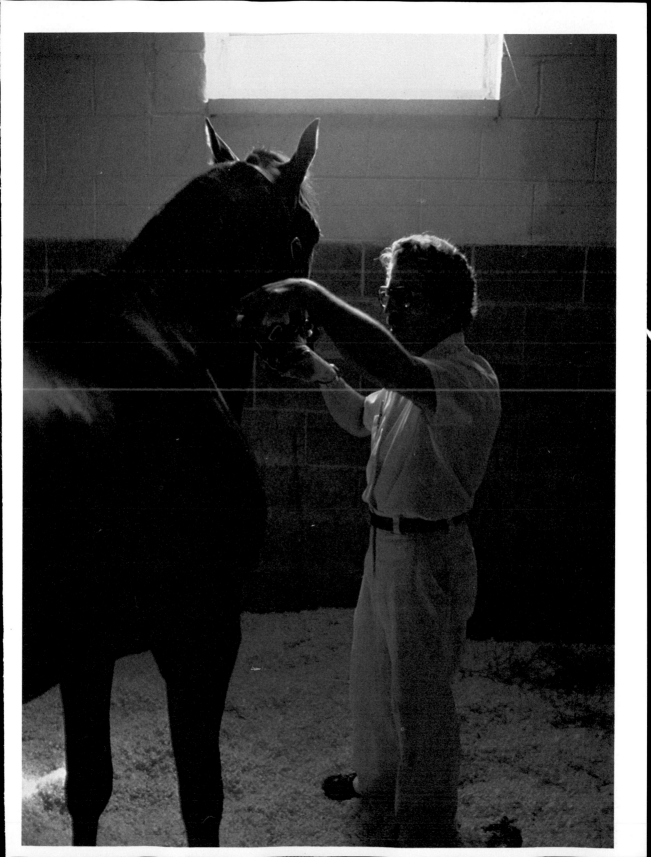

Is it hard to get into veterinary school?
You bet it is! There are only twenty-four accredited state colleges and three private veterinary colleges in the entire United States, and just three veterinary schools in Canada. There aren't enough schools to accommodate the number of students who apply for admission, and only a few more colleges of veterinary medicine are being planned.

For those lucky students who are admitted to a veterinary college, the basic education for equine doctors is the same as that for other veterinarians. It takes a total of six years of college—two and sometimes three years of pre-veterinary medicine plus four years in veterinary college—to earn the Doctor of Veterinary Medicine (D.V.M).

In order to practice, a person with a D.V.M. degree must pass a board examination and be issued a license by the state in which he or she plans to practice. Many doctors do post-graduate study or work in equine hospitals as interns to gain experience by assisting practicing veterinarians.

At the Illinois Equine Hospital, a graduate student is selected each year to live there and work as an intern. The hospital also accepts veterinary students who spend from three to six weeks observing hospital techniques.

Veterinary study requires effort; it isn't something you "breeze through." Students are required to learn hundreds of terms and remember a lot of information about animals and diseases. They must work in the laboratory and clinic to develop skill in diagnostic and surgical techniques.

Even after graduation veterinarians aren't finished learning. For as long as they practice, they must keep up-to-date with what's going on in their field.

Who makes a good equine veterinarian?
To become an equine veterinarian, you have to be in excellent health so you won't catch diseases that can be passed from horses to humans. You must be strong enough to handle a large animal and agile enough to move quickly if a horse tries to kick or step on you. Sharp vision and hearing are essential, as is good coordination. You also need an inquiring mind and strong powers of observation. Above all, it's important to understand horses and enjoy working with them.

Women in equine hospitals
Women on farms have always done a good job caring for animals. But for a long time it was thought that only men were capable of being veterinarians. Today it's agreed that women can do veterinary work as well as men.

The enrollment of women in veterinary school has tripled in recent years.

Men and women with the same qualifications have an equal chance of getting into veterinary school.

Besides working as veterinarians, women in equine hospitals are also animal technicians, laboratory technicians, barn and office workers, and barn managers.

The animal technician

The horse hospital health-care team involves many people who work under the supervision of the practicing veterinarian. Some have had formal schooling, others are given on-the-job training.

If you want a career in veterinary medicine but aren't interested in becoming a veterinarian, consider a career as an animal technician. You can begin training right after high school. Most animal technician training programs are two-year college level courses that involve academic study, practical experience with live animals, and training in routine laboratory and clinical work.

A technician's duties may include any part of the practice except diagnosis, prescription, surgery, and certain other activities prohibited by state law.

Scrubbing instruments is one of an animal technician's many jobs.

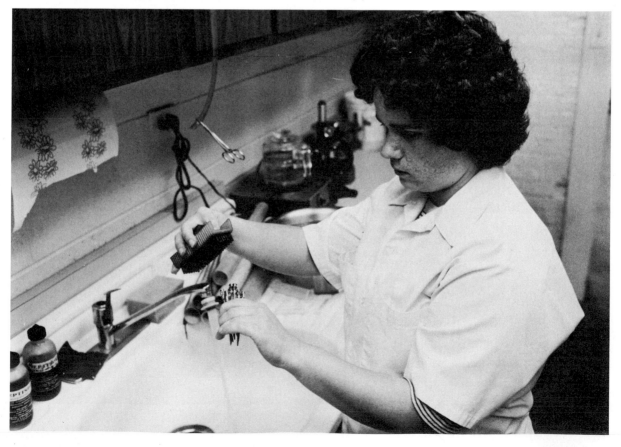

For example, technicians might prepare patients, instruments, and equipment for surgery. They may collect specimens and do routine laboratory work or expose and develop an X ray. They may file information and keep records. Technicians help give the doctor more time to spend with clients and patients.

When Ginger was being prepared for eye surgery at the Illinois Equine Hospital, a technician helped the doctors by selecting the surgical instruments and sterilizing them in an autoclave. Then Dr. Phillips and the other veterinarians were free to give Ginger an anesthetic and strap her to the operating table.

The barn workers

In large hospitals one of the barn workers is often appointed barn manager. The manager is responsible for the feed and shavings supply, and along with the other workers for keeping the stalls clean and the horses fed.

Ferrier George Collins puts the finishing touches on a patient's shoe. A horse's hoof, which is like a toenail, is so hard that the horse doesn't feel any pain when the shoe is nailed on.

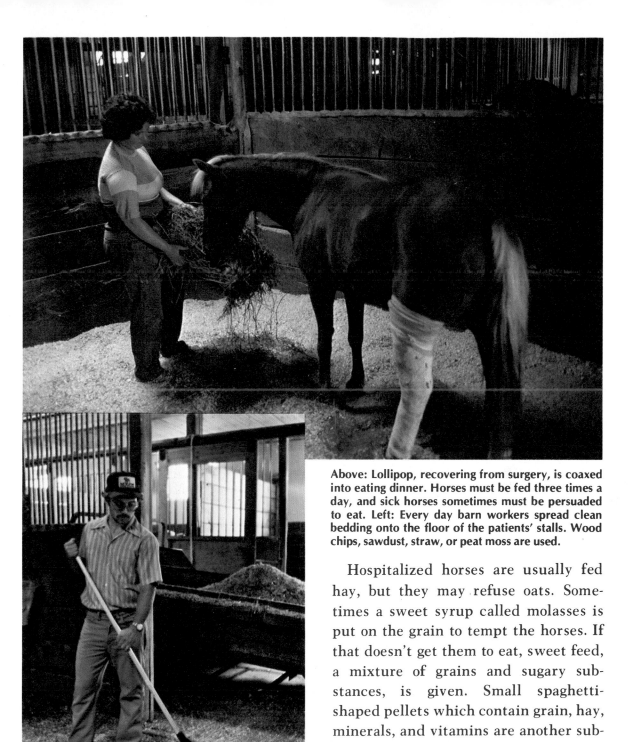

Above: Lollipop, recovering from surgery, is coaxed into eating dinner. Horses must be fed three times a day, and sick horses sometimes must be persuaded to eat. Left: Every day barn workers spread clean bedding onto the floor of the patients' stalls. Wood chips, sawdust, straw, or peat moss are used.

Hospitalized horses are usually fed hay, but they may refuse oats. Sometimes a sweet syrup called molasses is put on the grain to tempt the horses. If that doesn't get them to eat, sweet feed, a mixture of grains and sugary substances, is given. Small spaghetti-shaped pellets which contain grain, hay, minerals, and vitamins are another substitute for oats.

When necessary, vitamin supplements are put on the grain or squirted into the horse's mouth with a special rubber tube.

Barn workers fill the feed bins, water buckets, and hay racks. They put clean bedding in the stalls, keep the equipment in order, and watch the eating habits of the sick horses.

When a horse is on the mend, a worker may take him to the turnout and exercise him on a lunge line. The best part of the job is seeing a sick horse begin to "feel his oats."

When the lame pony from the handicapped riding class began to arch her back and kick up her heels, her barn worker threw his hat in the air and hollered, "Yipee!" The pony turned her head and gave the most tremendous whinny he'd ever heard. They celebrated the happy moment together.

A barn worker's job is mostly routine. But there are times when he or she might be able to help save a patient's life.

Miss Nancy King is a Quarter Horse who was hospitalized for kidney failure. The little mare had so much pain that she was unable to stand. She refused to eat or drink. The veterinarian prescribed medicine, and a barn worker was told to watch her.

It was winter and the barn was cold. The horse's temperature fell below normal, so the barn worker wrapped her in an electric blanket to keep her warm.

In spite of the blanket, Miss Nancy King was getting weaker. The medicine she had been given just wasn't working.

The barn worker alerted the veterinarian. After examining his patient, the doctor prescribed kanamycin. This antibiotic was not stocked at the equine hospital, so a nearby human hospital was contacted, and the medicine was obtained there.

The doctor stayed at the hospital and shot the antibiotic into the mare's veins at regular intervals during the night. The barn worker was right beside the doctor, tending the sick horse.

The next day, Miss Nancy King lifted her head, drank some water, and nibbled her feed. She was on her way to recovery.

There's a lot of dirty work connected with barn workers' jobs. They clean the surgical room after surgery and disinfect the isolation stall when a horse who had an infectious disease goes home. They have the smelly job of mucking out manure and wet bedding from the stalls. If there's a lull, there are always cobwebs to sweep.

But most barn workers feel that the good outweighs the bad. Their love of horses keeps them on the job.

The building engineer

Large hospitals usually have a building engineer on the staff who is in charge of keeping the building and grounds in good condition. The engineer and his helpers handle everything from planting trees to repairing broken stall doors.

Small hospitals might employ a part-time handyman instead of a building engineer and call in an expert for a major repair job.

In addition to doing usual maintenance work, the engineer at the Pompano Equine Clinic in Florida supervises the horses' swimming pool. Daily care is required to keep it sanitary. The water is tested periodically for bacteria. Every two months the old water is completely pumped out, filters are removed, and chlorine is added to clean water.

Since the pool is the only therapy for many horses at the clinic, the engineer's job is vital to their recovery.

The office staff

Without good office workers a horse hospital would not run smoothly. Office

Keeping the barn filled with hay is just one of Bob Phillips's many responsibilities as building engineer at the Illinois Equine Hospital.

Office workers keep track of records and provide vital communication between horses' owners and the hospital staff. Here Arlene Malmborg and Dr. Wiseman consult about appointments.

workers make appointments, check in patients, post charges, send out bills, and prepare reports.

Besides handling these routine tasks, office personnel are often trained to give emergency advice. They sometimes tell a worried owner what to do for a sick horse until the doctor arrives. Or an owner may be advised by an office worker to bring the horse to the hospital without delay.

When Amara cut herself on barbed wire, the owner was told by an office worker to get the mare and her colt to the hospital immediately. Because of

quick attention to the horse's wounds, infection was avoided. The office worker's advice may have saved Amara's life.

Sometimes office workers in small hospitals are given on-the-job training by veterinarians. They become knowledgeable about feeding and caring for sick horses.

How to prepare for a career as a vet
If you want a career in equine medicine, take as many science courses as possible. Read everything you can about animals and veterinary work. The library has many books on these subjects.

You might apply for an after-school or

summer job in a horse hospital. You'll probably have to start out by doing dirty work like mucking out stalls. But the sights and sounds of an equine hospital are exciting, and you'll learn a lot by being around horses and watching the veterinarians and other staff members work. You can ask questions and get advice about your future.

The Illinois Equine Hospital hires part-time high school and college students to help out in the hospital. Beside doing barn work, they are taught to prepare surgical packs and care for surgical instruments.

Research

Horse hospital veterinarians aren't usually involved in research projects. Research is done by their colleagues who work for businesses, colleges, or government agencies. But occasionally private hospitals are asked to participate in research projects.

For instance, several years ago the Illinois Equine Hospital did a clinical study on a West German anesthetic that

Time to go home! It's a happy day when a patient is well enough to return to its owner.

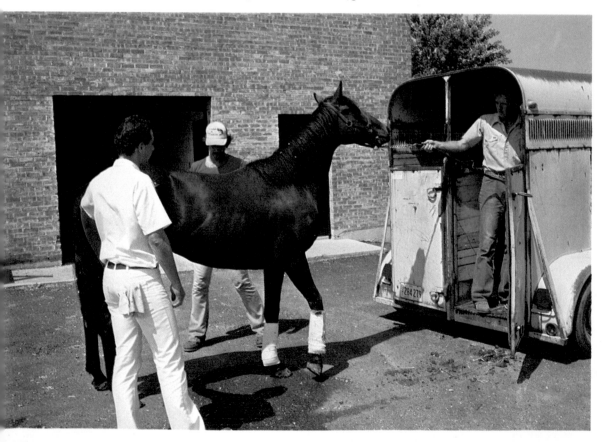

This may look like a lot of hay, but it won't last long. A healthy horse can eat about fourteen pounds of hay in one day. Barn cats keep a check on the mice who are attracted to the horses' feed. The big plastic bags contain wood shavings.

was not in use in the United States. And recently, the hospital tested a sulfa drug for a drug company.

A good place to work

The kind of veterinary medicine and surgery practiced in today's equine hospitals was almost unheard of before 1965. That's when the Illinois Equine Hospital opened its doors. It was one of the first privately owned hospitals in the country.

As more horse owners became interested in good health and long life for their valuable, loved animals, more hos-pitals were built. Today these hospitals and clinics have contributed much toward preventing illness and saving the lives of millions of sick animals. As health care institutions, equine hospitals are very effective.

Every worker, from veterinarian to barn attendant, plays an important role in caring for the patients. Perhaps some day you can work behind the scenes in an equine hospital.

There's a lot of satisfaction in seeing one of your patients walk out on his own four feet.

Glossary

anesthetic, a substance that dulls pain or causes sleep so pain cannot be felt.

abdominal cavity, the part of the body containing the stomach, intestines, and kidneys.

antibiotic, a substance that weakens or kills bacteria.

antihistamine, a kind of medicine used to treat allergies and colds.

Arabian, a popular, hardy breed of riding horse.

arthritis, a disease which causes swelling of the joints.

autoclave, a machine used to sterilize medical equipment.

bacteria, tiny organisms that can live in the bodies of animals and be either helpful or harmful to their health.

breeding, mating of two horses to produce a foal.

cancer, a sometimes fatal disease in which cells multiply out of control.

cauterization machine, a machine that uses heat to seal wounds or to destroy damaged tissue.

colic, severe abdominal cramping.

colon, a part of the large intestine.

colt, a male horse less than four years old.

cortisone, a medicine used to treat inflammations or allergies.

culture, the growth of bacteria from a sample of blood, urine, or tissue to determine the nature of the bacteria.

diagnosis, the identification of a health problem from its symptoms.

endoscopy, a medical procedure in which an interior part of the body is examined by looking through an instrument called an endoscope.

equine, having to do with horses.

Fallabella, the smallest breed of horse, only about thirty inches high.

ferrier, a person who makes and fits shoes for horses.

formaldehyde, a gas that can be put in a solution and used as a disinfectant and preservative.

foal, a newborn or very young male or female horse.

forceps, a medical instrument used for grasping and holding.

gamma rays, powerful electromagnetic rays that can be used to treat cancer or in X-ray machines to produce photographs of the interior of the body.

gelding, a male horse who has had some of its reproductive organs removed and cannot sire, or father, a foal.

histopathologist, a doctor who studies diseased and abnormal cells.

hock, a joint midway up the hind leg of a horse.

inflammation, an area of tissue that is red, hot, and swollen.

intern, a recent graduate of medical school who is working in a hospital to gain practical experience.

kanamycin, a kind of antibiotic.

kidney, an organ that processes waste matter from the body.

larynx, the part of the air passage in the throat that contains the voice box.

lunge line, a long rope used to exercise a horse.

lymph vessels, small vessels in the body that carry fluids to tissues and the blood.

mallet, a hammer with a wooden head.

mare, a female horse.

membrane, a layer of tissue that connects or separates parts of the body.

necropsy, the examination of an animal's body to determine the cause of death.

organism, any kind of living individual, including tiny bacteria.

oxygen, a colorless, tasteless, odorless gas necessary to the life of almost all living things.

parasite, an animal or plant that lives off of another live organism.

pathologist, a doctor who studies diseases.

penicillin, a medicine used to treat diseases caused by certain bacteria.

peritonitis, the swelling of the membrane that lines the abdominal walls.

pneumonia, a disease of the lungs.

purebred, a horse that has been bred from horses of the same breed.

Quarter Horse, a popular breed of horse used for riding.

radon, radioactive material that gives out gamma rays, used in the treatment of cancer.

scalpel, a small knife used in surgery.

stallion, a male horse.

Standardbred, a breed of horse that is often used for harness racing.

sterile, clean; free from germs.

strangles, a serious, highly contagious disease that affects a horse's breathing.

sulfa, a medicine used to stop the growth of bacteria.

tendon, a strong band of tissue that connects a muscle to a bone or other body part.

Thoroughbred, a breed of horse that is high spirited, sensitive, and well suited to racing.

tissue bank, a collection of preserved tissue samples kept for study.

tranquilizer, a drug used to relieve tension or reduce discomfort.

traction, the use of special equipment to exert a pulling force on parts of the skeleton.

turnout, an enclosed, circular area used for exercising horses.

vaccine, a solution made of killed or weakened bacteria or viruses. When injected, it causes the body to produce substances that can fight off disease.

X ray, a special ray that can penetrate the body so that a photograph of the interior can be made.

Index

Fern G. Brown is an avid horse person as well as an avid writer. When she's not working on a new book or visiting classrooms to encourage children to read and write, she may very well be found riding her Appaloosa, Woody Dip, over horse trails near her home in Deerfield, Illinois. Mrs. Brown also enjoys doing research and traveled around the United States to get information for *Behind the Scenes at the Horse Hospital*. She is the author of *Hard Luck Horse, You're Somebody Special on a Horse,* and *Jockey—or Else!*

Roger Ruhlin brings enthusiasm and expertise to all his assignments. He has been taking pictures professionally for over thirty years, beginning as a news photographer for United Press International. Born and reared in Chicago, Mr. Ruhlin now lives in the nearby town of Barrington and works as a free-lance photographer. He expands his photograph collection through extensive travel. His pictures appear in *Behind the Scenes at the Zoo* and *Behind the Scenes at the Aquarium*.